STRIVE

MASTER STRATEGY WITH AGILITY

HOW TO ACTIVATE YOUR VISION & THRIVE AMIDST UNCERTAINTY

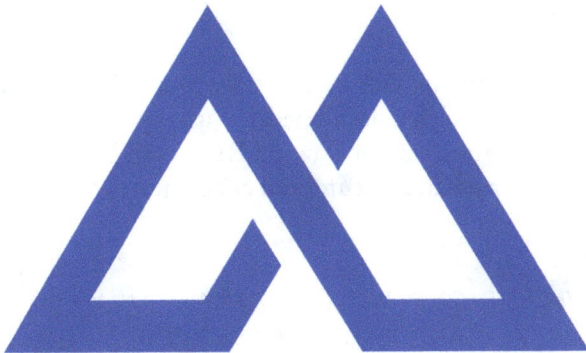

JONATHAN MAYO

STRIVE: MASTER STRATEGY WITH AGILITY

ADMINISTRATIVE PAGE

ISBN: 979-8-9876422-3-8 (paperback)
Publisher: Forge Publications

DISCLAIMER:

The information, methodologies, and strategies provided in the "STRIVE: Master Strategy with Agility" are for informational and educational purposes only. They are not intended to provide specific advice or recommendations for any individual or organization.

Iron Front Solutions and the author, Jonathan Mayo, make no representations or warranties with respect to the accuracy, applicability, fitness, or completeness of the contents of this handbook. The author and publisher disclaim any liability, loss, or risk taken by individuals who directly or indirectly act upon the information contained herein. All readers are encouraged to seek professional advice before making any decision that affects their business or financial standing.

By accessing and reading this handbook, you agree to accept the terms of this disclaimer.

The STRIVE Handbook outlines the core concepts and benefits of the STRIVE methodology developed for use by Iron Front Solutions. It serves to educate readers on how STRIVE can be applied to enable organizations to formulate, execute, and adapt strategy with agility.

This handbook was authored by Jonathan Mayo. The STRIVE methodology and contents of this handbook are the proprietary intellectual property of Jonathan Mayo for use through Iron Front Solutions.

Reproduction, distribution, or any other use of this handbook or the STRIVE methodology without express written consent of Iron Front Solutions is strictly prohibited.

FIRST EDITION: SEPTEMBER 2023

Iron Front Solutions
https://jonmayo.com

We welcome your feedback on this handbook as we continuously refine and expand on the STRIVE methodology.

FOREWORD

THE ORIGINS OF STRIVE: A METHODOLOGY FORGED FROM EXPERIENCE

Throughout my career leading organizations in both the military and civilian sectors, I have continuously sought to develop strategic frameworks that empower teams to accomplish ambitious goals. This passion stemmed from my hands-on leadership experience guiding units from the tactical and strategic levels as an Artillery Officer to managing business operations as an executive.

These roles immersed me in the intricacies and challenges of strategy - from executing on the frontlines to aligning stakeholders. Early on, I recognized the need for versatile yet structured approaches to strategic planning and execution suitable for the volatility of real life.

My initial leadership positions as a young Lieutenant directing Artillery fires as a Fire Supporter through my time as a Captain leading our Battalion's Fire Direction Center showed me first-hand the importance of situational awareness, risk management, and adaptability in chaotic environments. Mastering the technical complexities of coordinating indirect fires underscored the need for rigorous training and effective outcomes measurement.

Transitioning to the business world as a District Manager opened my eyes to cross-functional collaboration, continuous improvement, and fostering cultures empowered with autonomy and purpose. Moreover, spearheading process enhancements as a Lean Six Sigma Practitioner ingrained in me the potency of metrics, feedback loops, and systems thinking.

By the time I stepped into executive roles directing large-scale change initiatives, these experiences converged into several formative insights:

1. Strategies must be vigorously informed by data yet flexible enough to adjust amidst adversity or to changes in the operating environment. Neither rigidity nor reactionism by themselves are sufficient.

2. Visions and plans energize teams, but only when activated through individual ownership and engagement at every level.

3. In dynamic conditions, competitive advantage stems from learning velocity - how rapidly we gather insights, test new approaches, and course correct based on outcomes.

4. Leadership is not just planning but sculpting adaptive cultures committed to shared goals. This cultivates the agility required to secure the desired future at every level.

These insights shaped my conviction in developing STRIVE - to craft a strategic methodology blending analytical rigor with empathetic design and continuous adaptation. A methodology that surgically focuses on activating human potential and accomplishing aggressive organizational goals in pursuit of a shared vision, versus mechanically imposing models.

By incorporating the most impactful principles learned from my leadership experiences and borrowing brilliance from a broad spectrum of research and other industries, I believe STRIVE offers organizations a blueprint for strategic leadership in turbulent times. It is the product of hard-earned experience - a practical toolkit for progressing from static planning to continuous evolution.

Now having founded Iron Front Solutions, I am blessed with the opportunity to actively apply STRIVE in service of others. The journey of a thousand miles begins with a single step. I am honored to walk this path with ambitious leaders working to unleash their organizations' full potential. Are you ready? For at the intersection of challenge and purpose, transformation awaits.

TABLE OF CONTENTS

THE NEED FOR STRATEGIC AGILITY

"STRIVE helps Visionaries bring their Visions to life."

THE GROWING IMPERATIVE FOR STRATEGIC AGILITY

In an increasingly complex world of business, even industry giants find customary strategic planning models straining at the seams. Annual reviews and rigid Gantt charts rarely match the pace of disruption.

This leaves enterprises struggling on two fronts:

1. Formulating robust strategies amidst uncertainty.
2. Responsive execution in dynamic conditions.

Without agile frameworks, companies either handcuff themselves to legacy processes or resort to reactionary changes.

Organizations can no longer afford delayed responses given compressed innovation cycles and data-fueled startups rewriting competitive dynamics. The need for strategic agility has become an imperative.

INTRODUCING STRIVE - A BLUEPRINT FOR LEADING THROUGH UNCERTAINTY

The STRIVE methodology empowers organizations to operate at the speed of disruption through:

Structured Analysis: Tools like SWOT and Scenario Planning provide rigor yet adaptability to formulate strategies fit for volatility.

Agile Activation: Iterative planning techniques bridge the execution gap for long-term vision.

Responsive Execution: Embedded feedback loops foster on-the-fly adjustments through transparency.

With decades of multidisciplinary research synthesized into its adaptive design, STRIVE gives organizations a resilient blueprint for strategic leadership amidst uncertainty.

It is the missing link for impactful strategy - a platform that enables organizations to construct robust plans yet retain the versatility to adjust on the fly.

Change waits for no one. Playing catch up today means losing ground tomorrow. Succeeding amid uncertainty demands strategic agility - with both the vision to anticipate market shifts, the nimbleness to adapt on the fly, and the courage to take decisive action.

This is precisely what STRIVE delivers:

1. An integrated framework to formulate robust plans unencumbered by legacy structures.
2. An accelerated pathway to outmaneuver rivals too set in conventional thinking.
3. A resilient blueprint to master the future rather than merely survive it.

The opportunity for agility is now. The choice is yours - will you remain rigid or become resilient with STRIVE?

APPLYING STRIVE

AN ADAPTABLE METHODOLOGY

The STRIVE methodology is designed as an adaptable framework that can be customized to each organization's distinct context, goals, and requirements. Rather than a rigid, one-size-fits-all solution, it provides a flexible baseline that can be tailored and iteratively updated based on real-world inputs.

BRIDGING PLANNING WITH EXECUTION

STRIVE swiftly bridges the gap between planning and activation through iterative approaches. Intensive workshops and agile assessments generate insights while building consensus to inform executable strategies.

THE ITERATIVE STRIVE JOURNEY

Aligned assessments and workshops evaluate the current state, craft future aspirations, and identify priority areas to drive progress. Embedded Engage mechanisms also enable sustained, real-time learning and strategy improvement post-workshops.

CONTINUOUS FEEDBACK AND FINE-TUNING

Post-workshop, the focus turns to iteration based on operational feedback. Swift feedback cycles with stakeholders facilitate continuous fine-tuning to ensure responsiveness to market conditions.

THE ESSENCE OF STRIVE

STRIVE provides organizations a clear, adaptable pathway to realize their full potential. At its core, iterative assessment, planning, and correction makes STRIVE a guiding methodology for strategic leadership amid uncertainty.

STRIVE METHODOLOGY OVERVIEW

SITUATION (S)
ASSESS THE CURRENT STATE

Having a keen understanding of the current Situation enables organizations to build agility and continuously adapt strategy based on real-world insights.

"Know where you stand today."

OVERVIEW

The Situation assessment establishes the internal baseline by conducting analyses like SWOT, competitor profiling, customer segmentation and value chain mapping. This helps paint a picture of the organization's current state.

RETURN ON INVESTMENT (ROI)
OF SITUATION (S)

Thoroughly assessing your organization's current Situation will equip your leadership team with clarity on internal strengths, weaknesses, capabilities, and vulnerabilities. It enables data-driven competitor and market analysis to reveal where you truly stand. With this foundation of insights, you can make strategic decisions anchored in current realities rather than assumptions. Situational clarity provides the launchpad for everything that follows in the STRIVE methodology.

TRENDS (T)
ANTICIPATE MARKET SHIFTS

Diligently tracking Trends arms organizations with the foresight and external perspective to continuously adapt strategies in line with market forces and opportunities.

"Understand and monitor market shifts; catalyze innovation."

OVERVIEW

The Trends assessment examines the external dynamics that may impact the organization through environmental scanning, scenario planning, and identifying innovation opportunities. The goal is to anticipate potential industry shifts by identifying the Most Likely Trajectory (MLT), Most Dangerous Trajectory (MDT), and Most Preferred Trajectory (MPT).

RETURN ON INVESTMENT (ROI) OF TRENDS (T)

Diligently examining external Trends arms your organization with strategic foresight to stay ahead of market shifts. Assessment of political, economic, social, technological, and legal factors reveals signals of change that can significantly influence your industry. This understanding allows you to anticipate, prepare, and respond rather than just react. Tracking Trends also highlights "blue sky" where innovation can fuel growth. The Trends element enables you to intentionally shape your future.

RISKS (R)
OVERCOME RIGIDITY WITH RISK PLANNING

Proactively evaluating Risks provides the confidence and agility to swiftly adapt strategies in the face of new challenges.

"Transform uncertainty into opportunity; risks provide the fuel for agility."

OVERVIEW

The Risks assessment identifies and evaluates potential challenges and vulnerabilities through market threat analysis, regulatory compliance reviews, and operational audits. This highlights areas of risk exposures.

RETURN ON INVESTMENT (ROI) OF RISKS (R)

Rigorously evaluating Risks provides visibility into exposures that could impede the strategic trajectory. Exploration of market threats, regulatory shifts and internal operational risks highlights areas of vulnerability. But crucially, this assessment enables preemptively fortifying against downside scenarios. Risk mitigation also builds strategic confidence to pursue bold moves knowing potential pitfalls are covered. Managing and/or accepting risks provides fuel for agility that transforms contingencies into intentional maneuver.

INTENT (I)

Establishing clear Intent enables organizations to activate strategy with a North Star to guide agile execution.

> "Define your vision, set your milestones, and measure as you move."

OVERVIEW

The Intent exercise outlines the destination by crafting or refining vision and mission statements. It plots critical milestones by defining strategic objectives and Key Performance Indicators (KPIs) to track progress. This brings clarity and alignment.

RETURN ON INVESTMENT (ROI) OF INTENT (I)

Defining your organization's Intent establishes alignment and unity of effort. Crafting an inspirational vision backed by strategic objectives and progress metrics acts as a North Star guiding decisions and actions. With clear Intent, priorities become unambiguous, and teams can execute with autonomy knowing they are advancing the vision. Intent enables organizational effort to be leveraged for maximum impact.

VENTURE (V)

The Venture element empowers organizations to swiftly progress from planning to execution with flexible roadmaps that activate agile strategy.

> "Venture forth with purpose, picking the paths of utmost priority."

OVERVIEW

The Venture exercise maps the strategic path forward by identifying and prioritizing initiatives, projects and actions needed to achieve the vision and objectives. This creates a roadmap for execution that nests current actions in alignment with future goals.

RETURN ON INVESTMENT (ROI) OF VENTURE (V)

Mapping the Venture element of STRIVE crystallizes the strategic path forward drawing a critical path from the current state, through the vision established in Intent. Rigorously identifying and prioritizing key initiatives and actions creates a blueprint for execution. Venture action plans also enable teams to sequence and stage activities for optimal returns. Rather than just lofty ideas, this element of STRIVE provides an actionable roadmap to activate strategy.

ENGAGE (E)
ENABLE CONTINUOUS ADAPTATION

Embedding Engage into workflows fosters a culture of learning and adaptation, powering the agility to continuously evolve strategy.

> "Engage in continuous feedback, collaborate efficiently, and adapt when necessary."

OVERVIEW

The Engage element is the critical continuous improvement, consistency and accountability forcing function as it puts in place the mechanisms to sustain strategic change through feedback channels, collaboration tools and regular stakeholder reviews. This enables adaptation in response to shifting dynamics and ensures successful change.

RETURN ON INVESTMENT
(ROI) OF ENGAGE (E)

Embedding Engage into workflows fosters rapid learning and adaptation which is key to resilience. Continuous stakeholder feedback, real-time data, and regular strategy reviews enable live course correction versus rigid plans. Engage also operationalizes successful change through tools like prototyping and iteration. In dynamic environments, strategic agility enabled by Engage is a competitive advantage.

In summary, the STRIVE methodology provides an end-to-end strategic planning framework - from internal baseline setting, external analysis, risk planning, intent alignment, execution planning and engagement. The elements create a comprehensive and integrated strategic planning approach that, when applied, will transform aspirations into action, which is the only path to success.

MASTERING THE ART AND SCIENCE OF STRATEGY WITH THE STRIVE METHODOLOGY

In today's complex, technologically advanced, and ever-changing world, devising an astute strategy is no longer just a pursuit of profits – it is a prerequisite for relevance, growth, and even survival. Yet, crafting strategy involves far more than retrospective analysis or inspired ideation. Turning strategic thinking into strategic progress demands a robust framework that blends vision and action with agility and adaptation. This is where the STRIVE Methodology comes into play.

STRIVE offers organizations a structured yet flexible approach to developing, executing, and evolving strategy in a phased manner. The acronym itself elucidates the key elements that enable enterprises to progress from strategic planning to strategic leadership:

S - Situation - Gain clarity on where you stand today.

T - Trends - Identify market patterns, consumer shifts and emerging innovations.

R - Risks - Recognize potential challenges spanning operations, regulations, and competition.

I - Intent - Define a compelling vision, set objectives, and establish metrics.

V - Venture - Venture forth through prioritized, impactful actions linked to your vision.

E - Engage - Foster relentless feedback, agile teams, and continuous adaptation.

At its core, STRIVE provides the structure for organizations to achieve alignment between strategic insights and operational execution. The Situation and Trends elements enable evidence-based analysis of external environments and market forces while Risks highlights potential vulnerabilities. These foundations enable organizations to define their

Intent with clarity on their future vision, supporting objectives and progress metrics (KPIs).

But STRIVE's value extends beyond planning. With Venture, it steers organizations toward purposeful action. With Engage, it emphasizes continuous adaptation based on real-time assessments and stakeholder feedback. This fusion of strategy formulation and execution, complemented by agile adaptation, is the cornerstone of the methodology.

As a strategic framework, STRIVE interweaves prescriptive steps with adaptive principles, helping organizations chart their course amidst uncertainty while retaining the agility to adjust when required. The methodology blends time-tested strategic planning tools like SWOT analyses with more agile techniques like scenario planning and iterative feedback loops. This blend of structured analysis and flexible execution makes STRIVE broadly applicable across diverse organizational contexts while still offering customizable components tailored to unique needs.

In summary, the STRIVE Methodology offers more than just a process for developing strategy – it provides a pathway for organizations to progress from strategic planning to strategic leadership. Today, having the vision to craft smart strategy is just the beginning – you also need the versatility to steer your organization through ever-changing conditions. With its blended focus on strategic insights and agile execution, STRIVE gives organizations the tools not just to charter their course amidst uncertainty but also to achieve their goals regardless of how the winds may shift.

UNDERSTANDING THE STRIVE METHODOLOGY

SITUATION (S)

ASSESS THE CURRENT STATE

Having a keen understanding of the current Situation enables organizations to build agility and continuously adapt strategy based on real-world insights.

"Know where you stand today."

OVERVIEW

The Situation assessment establishes the internal baseline by conducting analyses like SWOT, competitor profiling, customer segmentation and value chain mapping. This helps paint a picture of the organization's current state.

RETURN ON INVESTMENT (ROI) OF SITUATION (S)

Thoroughly assessing your organization's current Situation will equip your leadership team with clarity on internal strengths, weaknesses, capabilities, and vulnerabilities. It enables data-driven competitor and market analysis to reveal where you truly stand. With this foundation of insights, you can make strategic decisions anchored in current realities rather than assumptions. Situational clarity provides the launchpad for everything that follows in the STRIVE methodology.

UNDERSTANDING THE POWER OF "SITUATION"

Navigation without first pinpointing one's exact position is like steering a ship blindfolded. For this reason, STRIVE begins with the SITUATION element. This foundational component urges organizations to gain a comprehensive understanding of their current circumstances before continuing forward, ensuring decisions are both grounded and strategic.

The importance of truly grasping the "Situation" is made clearer through Simon Sinek's philosophy of 'Starting with Why'. To craft a coherent and impactful strategy, establishing a clear baseline understanding is paramount. From this vantage point, organizations are not only informed about the present but are also better equipped to anticipate the future.

Illustrating this principle, various sectors underline the significance of understanding the "Situation":

1. **Psychology:** The pathway to personal growth in therapeutic disciplines like Cognitive Behavioral Therapy starts with self-awareness. It is pivotal for patients to discern and challenge maladaptive thought patterns, laying the groundwork for meaningful transformation.

2. **Business:** Companies regularly assess their performance relative to competitors and industry norms. For example, Toyota's Just-In-Time manufacturing innovation was born from a keen understanding of their marketplace standing.

3. **Education:** Educational institutions use standardized tests to measure students' baseline capabilities. With insights about where students currently stand, educators can optimize learning materials and teaching strategies for maximum efficacy.

4. **Military:** In defense and strategy, successful military operations hinge on comprehensive reconnaissance. By deeply examining current conditions, including the lay of the land and opponent capabilities, commanders formulate strategies that capitalize on strengths and minimize vulnerabilities.

The Situation element extends beyond simply taking stock of the present. It involves leveraging tools like SWOT analyses to genuinely understand an organization's strengths, weaknesses, opportunities, and threats. This detailed assessment enables companies to harness their strengths, address weaknesses, seize opportunities, and defend against threats.

In conclusion, the "Situation" component is undeniably central to the STRIVE methodology and, by extension, to successful strategic planning. Regardless of the industry – whether it is personal growth, business innovation, educational advancements, or military operations – the principle remains the same: truly understanding where you are now is the key to determining where you should go next, as well as how to best get there. Given this, having a robust understanding of one's Situation is not just beneficial; it is an absolute necessity.

SITUATION (S) EXERCISES

Purpose: Ground your strategic efforts in a clear understanding of your present circumstances.

EXERCISE 1:
CURRENT STATE ANALYSIS

Objective: Paint a vivid picture of where your organization stands today, highlighting strengths, weaknesses, and identifying opportunities and threats.

Method: SWOT + Customer and Competitor Analysis

SWOT ANALYSIS

1. **STRENGTHS**
   - What internal assets (people, intellectual property, etc.) give us an edge?
   - What operational processes work particularly well?

2. **WEAKNESSES**
   - Which processes need refinement or rethinking?
   - Are there gaps in our skills or resources?

3. **OPPORTUNITIES**
   - Which market gaps can we potentially fill?
   - Are there partnerships or collaborations that could amplify our reach?

4. **THREATS**
   - What internal challenges could impact us?
   - What elephants are in the room that we have been ignoring for too long?

COMPETITOR ANALYSIS

1. Who are our 3 biggest competitors by market share?
2. What are their competitive advantages or differentiators?
3. What customer needs do they serve best?

CUSTOMER SEGMENTATION ANALYSIS

1. How can we categorize customers into distinct segments based on needs, behaviors, demographics etc.?
2. Which segments offer the most growth potential?
3. Which segments should we prioritize serving (if necessary, rate responses for this response)?

EXERCISE 2:
INTERNAL VALUE CHAIN ANALYSIS

Objective: Assess the company's key capabilities and resources across their value chain.

Method: Value Chain Mapping & Analysis

VALUE CHAIN ANALYSIS

1. Map out the key activities, resources, and capabilities across the company's primary value chain, consider:

   - Inbound logistics (sourcing, procurement)
   - Operations
   - Outbound logistics
   - Marketing & sales
   - Service

2. Analyze the support functions/capabilities that enable the primary value chain:

   - → HR
   - → Procurement
   - → R&D
   - → Infrastructure etc.

3. Identify advantages or gaps in capabilities.

   - → Where do we have strengths to leverage?
   - → Where are the capability gaps, we need to address?

KEY TAKEAWAYS

1. Gained clarity on internal strengths, weaknesses, opportunities, and threats through SWOT analysis.

2. Mapped internal capabilities and potential competitive advantages through Value Chain Analysis.

3. Developed comprehensive profile of our organizations current state to inform strategic planning.

TAKE IT FURTHER

1. Review this worksheet at regular intervals, especially post major industry events or internal organizational shifts. The landscape can change rapidly, and revisiting and revising your understanding of your Situation ensures you remain agile and prepared.

2. Encourage a culture of continuous learning and iterative improvement as you navigate through the STRIVE framework. The key to the success of any methodology is its consistent application and the willingness of the team to engage in open, honest reflection.

TRENDS (T)

ANTICIPATE MARKET SHIFTS

Diligently tracking Trends arms organizations with the foresight and external perspective to continuously adapt strategies in line with market forces and opportunities.

> "Understand and monitor market shifts; catalyze innovation."

OVERVIEW

The Trends assessment examines the external dynamics that may impact the organization by doing environmental scanning, scenario planning, and identifying innovation opportunities. The goal is to anticipate potential industry shifts by identifying the Most Likely Trajectory (MLT), Most Dangerous Trajectory (MDT), and Most Preferred Trajectory (MPT).

RETURN ON INVESTMENT (ROI) OF TRENDS (T)

Diligently examining external Trends arms your organization with strategic foresight to stay ahead of market shifts. Assessment of political, economic, social, technological, and legal factors reveals signals of change that can significantly influence your industry. This understanding allows you to anticipate, prepare, and respond rather than just react. Tracking Trends also highlights white spaces where innovation can fuel growth. The Trends element enables you to intentionally shape your future.

TRENDS: AN EXAMINATION ACROSS INDUSTRIES

Maintaining a competitive advantage necessitates more than just proactive decisions. It requires a profound understanding of shifting market dynamics and a readiness to evolve with them. Central to this is the "TRENDS" element of the STRIVE framework, which underscores the strategic value of recognizing and harnessing market patterns to drive innovation and maintain competitiveness.

TUNING INTO TRENDS: A STRATEGIC IMPERATIVE

Harnessing market trends is not about jumping on every new fad. At its heart, it means engaging actively with the external environment, blending the analytical process of assessing market dynamics with the creative act of uncovering untapped potentials. This approach equips organizations with a forward-looking perspective, enabling them to seize emerging opportunities before competitors even spot them.

THE VALUE OF TRENDS: PERSPECTIVES FROM VARIOUS SECTORS

1. **Business:** The tale of Blockbuster and Netflix vividly illustrates the consequences of trend recognition. While Blockbuster's oversight of digital streaming's potential led to its downfall, Netflix's foresight and adaptation heralded its explosive rise in the entertainment industry.

2. **Psychology:** Dr. Carol Dweck's research on 'Growth Mindset' offers insights into how beliefs shape actions. Translated to market trends, it becomes clear that organizations with a 'fixed' mindset may resist change, while those with a 'growth' mindset view trends as avenues for innovation. The global shift towards lifelong learning

exemplifies this, as educational institutions now offer extensive online courses to cater to evolving student needs.

3. **Military:** As warfare has evolved, so have military tactics. Traditional strategies were often ill-prepared for modern challenges like guerrilla warfare and cyber threats. Recognizing such trends, contemporary military doctrines emphasize flexibility and adaptability, necessitating the inclusion of cyber and space components within our armed forces.

4. **Healthcare:** The trend toward telemedicine, especially accelerated by the COVID-19 pandemic, exemplifies healthcare's adaptive nature. Institutions that embraced telehealth not only met urgent demands but also expanded into new market niches, while those resistant risked becoming outdated.

MARKET ANALYSIS AND INNOVATION: THE DUAL FACES OF TRENDS

Effectively harnessing trends involves two pivotal steps:

1. MARKET DYNAMICS ANALYSIS

Tools like the Iron Front's Focused PESTLE Analysis help capture the inclination and direction of the times, offering insights into various market-shaping factors, from political shifts to technological innovations. But beyond data collection, the goal is to delve into the nuances that often herald significant market shifts.

2. OPPORTUNITIES EXPLORATION

Recognizing a trend is just the starting point. The next phase involves brainstorming sessions to transition from observation to ideation. This proactive exploration seeks to integrate trends into business strategies, pinpoint market gaps, and envision transformative products or solutions.

IN CONCLUSION

The TRENDS component of the STRIVE framework amplifies the essence of proactive market awareness in strategic planning. It is a clarion call for organizations to not only monitor but also anticipate and shape the trajectory of the market. In our rapidly changing world, understanding, and leveraging trends is not just beneficial—it is a strategic necessity for any organization aspiring to lead and thrive.

TRENDS (T) EXERCISES

Purpose: To identify core market trends and pinpoint high-impact innovation opportunities swiftly and efficiently.

EXERCISE 1:
FOCUSED MARKET DYNAMICS ANALYSIS

Objective: Understand current and emerging major market shifts and assess pivotal consumer behavior changes.

Method: Iron Front's Focused PESTLE Analysis (Political, Economic, Social, Technological, Legal, Environmental)

IRON FRONT'S FOCUSED PESTLE ANALYSIS

1. POLITICAL & LEGAL

- ➔ Prioritize major political and legal changes with direct industry implications.
- ➔ Are there any political factors that might influence the market?
- ➔ Upcoming elections, political stability, foreign relations, etc.
- ➔ Are there upcoming legal changes or regulations that could affect your business?
- ➔ New laws, regulatory bodies, compliance standards, etc.

2. ECONOMIC

- ➔ Highlight significant economic indicators directly impacting your sector.
- ➔ What are the economic trends in your industry or region?
  - ➔ Economic growth, inflation rate, exchange rates, etc.

3. SOCIAL & ENVIRONMENTAL

- Focus on key societal shifts and major environmental concerns.
- How are societal attitudes and behaviors shifting?
  - Population growth, age distribution, cultural attitudes, etc.
- Any environmental or sustainability trends to be aware of?
  - Climate change, sustainability initiatives, green technologies, etc.

4. TECHNOLOGICAL

- Identify core technological advancements with immediate relevance.
- What are the technological advancements affecting the industry?
  - New platforms, tools, apps, software, AI, etc.

BRING IT TOGETHER

1. Given the above, what is the Most Preferred Trajectory (MPT), Most Likely Trajectory (MLT), and Most Dangerous Trajectory (MDT) given our current stance (from Situation) and Trend analysis? Capture these three items in one sentence statements.

2. Brainstorm: What is one action that comes to the top of your mind that we can take to shift our trajectory from MLT and MDT to MPT?

EXERCISE 2:
TARGETED INNOVATION OPPORTUNITIES EXPLORATION

Objective: Pinpoint key innovation areas directly aligned with identified high-impact trends.

Method: Guided Brainstorming Session

1. **TREND APPLICATION**
   - For each identified trend from exercise 1, discuss potential applications for your business.
   - How can we leverage this trend to our advantage?

2. **GAP ANALYSIS**
   - Look at the current market offerings. Are there gaps that you can fill with innovative solutions?
   - Now eliminate all but 3 major market gaps offering the most potential.

3. **BLUE SKY THINKING**
   - For the 3 major market offering gaps:
     - Without constraints, what would the ideal solution or product look like?
     - Encourage creativity and out-of-the-box thinking.
     - Narrow down the list by prioritizing feasible, high-impact ideas, always relating back to the core trends identified.

KEY TAKEAWAYS

1. Identified major shifts and dynamics in the external environment through Iron Front's Focused PESTLE analysis.

2. Pinpointed key innovation opportunities aligned to market trends and gaps.

3. Identified potential future trajectories and growth opportunities.

TAKE IT FURTHER

1. Synthesize insights into an executive overview spotlighting the most impactful trends and potential innovations. This becomes an agile guiding document for strategy activation.

2. Maintain a supplemental catalog of all trend data gathered. Revisit regularly for continued analysis as the landscape evolves.

3. Allow the distilled insights to guide the Intent, Venture and Engage phases. Continuously realign as new information emerges.

4. Treat the Trends overview as a living document, not a fixed endpoint. Use it to drive an ongoing process of trend monitoring, opportunity validation and strategic evolution.

RISKS (R)

OVERCOME RIGIDITY WITH RISK PLANNING

Proactively evaluating Risks provides the confidence and agility to swiftly adapt strategies in the face of new challenges.

"Transform uncertainty into opportunity; risks provide the fuel for agility."

OVERVIEW

The Risks assessment identifies and evaluates potential challenges and vulnerabilities through market threat analysis, regulatory compliance reviews, and operational audits. This highlights areas of risk exposures.

RETURN ON INVESTMENT (ROI) OF RISKS (R)

Rigorously evaluating Risks provides visibility into exposures that could impede the strategic trajectory. Exploration of market threats, regulatory shifts and internal operational risks highlights areas of vulnerability. But crucially, this assessment enables preemptively fortifying against downside scenarios. Risk mitigation also builds strategic confidence to pursue bold moves knowing potential pitfalls are covered. Managing and/or accepting risks provides fuel for agility.

STRATEGIC RISK MANAGEMENT WITH STRIVE

The "RISKS" element of the STRIVE framework heralds the call for organizations to not only be vigilant against potential pitfalls but to proactively turn them into steppingstones for growth and innovation.

UNDERSTANDING THE ESSENCE OF RISK

The STRIVE methodology elucidates risk management as more than just a reactive measure. It is a proactive strategy aimed at staying ahead, continually evaluating internal vulnerabilities and external threats to craft an adaptive and resilient roadmap. Through the lens of STRIVE, risks become not just challenges to overcome but opportunities to innovate and grow stronger.

Here are a few lessons from the frontlines to consider:

1. **Tech:** The BlackBerry saga serves as a poignant lesson on the repercussions of failing to anticipate market shifts. While it once was the dominant player in mobile communication, BlackBerry was outpaced by competitors who foresaw and embraced the smartphone revolution, illuminating the perils of complacency and resistance to change.

2. **Education:** The "Sunk Cost Fallacy" in educational institutions highlights the dangers of adhering to outdated systems due to previous investments, sidelining the escalating risks of becoming obsolete in a tech-forward world.

3. **Military:** The attack on Pearl Harbor stands as a grim testament to the grave consequences of underestimating clear and present dangers, underscoring the significance of vigilance and adaptive strategy.

4. **Automotive:** Volkswagen's 'Dieselgate' scandal showcases the immense risks of non-compliance, spotlighting the dire need for upholding regulatory mandates and ethical practices.

A STRUCTURED APPROACH TO RISK MANAGEMENT

STRIVE's risk module champions a three-sided approach:

1. **Market Threats Assessment:** By utilizing insights from the Situation and Trends elements of STRIVE, as well as by employing tools such as a Risk Focused SWOT analysis, organizations can swiftly externalize their gaze, pinpointing potential challenges from competitors, supply chain vulnerabilities, and changing consumer behaviors.

2. **Regulatory and Compliance Review:** STRIVE emphasizes not just adherence to current standards but anticipates potential shifts, ensuring businesses remain compliant and safeguard their reputational capital.

3. **Operational Audit:** Delving into the operational core, STRIVE assists organizations in recognizing their strengths and weaknesses, bolstered by insights from those at the ground level—employees.

IN CONCLUSION

In the STRIVE methodology, risks are reframed from mere challenges to be tackled into transformative opportunities. Its structured approach ensures that businesses not only mitigate risks but leverage them as catalysts for growth, innovation, and sustainable progress. In a world rife with uncertainties, STRIVE empowers organizations to not just navigate risks but harness them.

RISKS (R) EXERCISES

Purpose: To methodically uncover, scrutinize, and rank potential challenges which might influence the organization's trajectory. This includes both external market challenges and potential internal operational vulnerabilities.

EXERCISE 1:
MARKET THREATS ASSESSMENT

Objective: Gain clarity on external challenges that could affect business growth or stability.

Method: Focused SWOT Analysis (Concentrating on Threats)

RISK FOCUSED SWOT ANALYSIS

1. **COMPETITOR LANDSCAPE**

   ⊙ Identify new entrants or emerging competitors in the market.

   ⊙ What are their unique selling propositions? How do they differentiate from our offerings?

2. **CONSUMER BEHAVIOR AND PREFERENCES**

   ⊙ Capture evolving consumer behaviors, needs, or preferences.

   ⊙ Are there untapped or emerging market segments?

3. **SUPPLY CHAIN DYNAMICS**

   ⊙ Highlight potential factors or events that could destabilize the supply chain.

   ⊙ Account for geopolitical dynamics, environmental factors, labor issues, etc.

EXERCISE 2:
REGULATORY & COMPLIANCE SCAN

Objective: Continuously remain aligned with regulatory shifts and ensure rigorous compliance.

Method: Comprehensive Regulatory Review

1. FORECASTED REGULATORY SHIFTS

- ➔ Are there imminent or proposed regulatory changes that could impact operations?
- ➔ Foster ties with industry bodies and think tanks for early warnings.

2. CURRENT COMPLIANCE HEALTH CHECK

- ➔ Assess and benchmark current processes against prevailing regulatory requirements.
- ➔ Pinpoint areas of potential misalignment or compliance vulnerabilities.

EXERCISE 3:
DELVE INTO OPERATIONAL INSIGHTS

Objective: Delineate operational robustness and pinpoint areas of potential vulnerability.

Method: High Level Operational Audit

1. OPERATIONAL PILLARS

⊙ Recognize facets where operational processes shine.

⊙ Could these facets be spotlighted as unique value propositions or competitive edges?

⊙ Is there something that could change this that has been left unaddressed?

2. POTENTIAL CHINKS IN THE ARMOR

⊙ What real or potential fragilities or inefficiencies are lurking within operations?

⊙ Consider aspects such as technology redundancy, manual bottlenecks, skill gaps, or infrastructural vulnerabilities.

ADDITIONAL RESOURCE: GROUND-LEVEL FEEDBACK

1. Tap into the perspective of frontline personnel for unvarnished, ground-level insights. Their experiential knowledge can be invaluable.

2. Consider tools like anonymous feedback boxes or structured interviews to gather data.

3. Conducting analysis like this and allowing it to inform your efforts in the Engage element of STRIVE will help to further enhance the team's effectiveness.

KEY TAKEAWAYS

1. Assessed external threats, internal vulnerabilities and compliance gaps through SWOT analysis and audits.

2. Developed prioritized risk profile to inform exposure management.

3. Gained visibility into challenges that could impede the strategic trajectory.

TAKE IT FURTHER

1. Synthesize data from all exercises to create a robust risk profile.

2. Prioritize actionable items, especially those associated with compliance and areas of high vulnerability.

3. Set up periodic review checkpoints to ensure risks are continually managed and mitigated, not just initially identified.

4. For high-risk areas, develop contingency plans to ensure the organization remains agile and resilient in the face of unforeseen challenges.

INTENT (I)

Establishing clear Intent enables organizations to activate strategy with a North Star to guide agile execution.

"Define your vision, set your milestones, and measure as you move."

OVERVIEW

The Intent exercise outlines the destination by crafting or refining vision and mission statements. It identifies critical milestones by defining strategic objectives and KPIs to track progress. This brings clarity and alignment.

RETURN ON INVESTMENT (ROI) OF INTENT (I)

Defining your organization's Intent establishes alignment and focus. Crafting an inspirational vision backed by strategic objectives and progress metrics acts as a North Star guiding decisions and actions. With clear Intent, priorities become unambiguous, and teams can execute with autonomy knowing they are advancing the vision. Intent enables organizational effort to be leveraged for maximum impact.

DRIVING PROGRESS WITH INTENT

"Intent" captures the essence of an organization's purpose and crystallizes its ambitions into actionable objectives. Intent serves as the bedrock for constructing strategies, outlining objectives, and bringing visions to fruition. STRIVE is meticulously designed to cultivate a well-informed approach, bridging the gap between aspirations, realization and emphasizing its paramount significance across various industries. But the importance of Intent extends beyond procedure; it is the very foundation upon which progress is measured and visions are realized.

HERE IS WHY:

1. **Tech and Business:** Apple's ascendancy in the tech world was not just the product of innovation but rooted in a clear intent—merging humanities with technology. Their vision, as articulated by Steve Jobs, moved beyond gadgets to experiences. This clarity of purpose positioned Apple at the vanguard of industry evolution.

2. **Education:** Howard Gardner's "Theory of Multiple Intelligences" emerged from a clear intent—to redefine how intelligence is perceived. It transformed educational paradigms, pushing institutions towards personalized learning approaches.

3. **Military:** The U.S. Military's pivot to Multi-Domain Operations underscores the adaptability required in recognizing and responding to threats. This evolutionary step was a manifestation of the military's unwavering intent—to protect and defend across multiple domains.

4. **Retail:** Amazon's trajectory is emblematic of the power of intent. With a mission to become the most customer-centric company on earth, every innovation, from Prime to Whole Foods, aligns with this intent, redefining the retail experience.

5. **Entrepreneurship:** Elon Musk's ventures, be it Tesla, SpaceX, Neuralink, Boring Company, SolarCity, or Starlink, echo a harmonized intent—innovating for a sustainable future. Each venture, while varied in its domain, resonates with Musk's overarching vision of creating a more sustainable and interconnected future.

ANATOMY OF STRATEGIC INTENT

At the heart of STRIVE's Intent module is a trifold approach to defining actionable Intent:

1. **Vision Crafting:** Envisioning the future, combining the organization's ethos with its aspirations.

2. **Setting Objectives:** Identifying tangible milestones that act as steppingstones towards the envisioned future, using SMART/ER criteria to ensure precision.

3. **KPI Establishment:** Harnessing metrics to measure the organization's progress (measure as you go), acting as the compass ensuring accurate alignment with the overarching vision.

IN CONCLUSION

The "Intent" facet of STRIVE does not just prescribe a set of steps; it provides the compass, the map, and the milestones for organizations navigating the complexities of their respective industries. It is the convergence of aspiration and preparation, as it prepares the way for execution. For businesses aiming to lead, innovate, and reshape their domains, aligning every step with a well-defined intent is the catalyst to accomplishing your goals and building a living legacy.

INTENT (I) EXERCISES

Purpose: To articulate a clear vision for the future, identify the immediate goals that will act as steppingstones towards that vision, and establish metrics to gauge the progress effectively.

EXERCISE 1:
VISION CRAFTING

Objective: Define a compelling vision for the future that aligns with the company's values, current situation, market trends, and risk profile.

Method: Vision Statement Development

VISION STATEMENT DEVELOPMENT

1. **REVIEW FINDINGS FROM PREVIOUS EXERCISES**
   - ⊛ Revisit key insights from the Situation, Trends, and Risks analysis.
   - ⊛ What strengths or weaknesses were identified?
   - ⊛ What potential opportunities or threats exist?

2. **DISTILL YOUR CORE VALUES**
   - ⊛ What values or purpose guide the company?
   - ⊛ What principles or beliefs shape culture and decisions?

3. **CONSIDER POTENTIAL TRAJECTORIES**
   - ⊛ What is the preferred future scenario and trajectory we want to realize?
   - ⊛ What is the most dangerous trajectory we want to avoid?

4. DRAFT THE VISION STATEMENT

→ Craft a concise vision statement that encapsulates the core values, accounts for current situation and trends, mitigates key risks, and sets the trajectory.

VISION CRAFTING:

Template for crafting vision statements:

→ [Core Purpose]: Why we exist; the meaningful impact we seek to make.

→ [Envisioned Future]: The ambitious yet grounded vision we aim to achieve.

→ [Core Values]: What guides our journey; principles that shape our culture.

Example:

"To unleash human potential globally [Core Purpose] by pioneering personalized, empowering education platforms [Envisioned Future] through a culture of innovation, empathy and conscious leadership [Core Values]."

Tips for an inspirational, achievable vision:

→ Root it in higher purpose - connect to meaningful impact.

→ Make it bold and aspirational while grounding it in strategic analysis.

→ Ensure it aligns with values and provides cultural continuity.

→ Balance ambition with practical milestones through objectives.

EXERCISE 2:
KPIS ESTABLISHMENT

Objective: Define metrics to track progress towards short-term objectives and the overarching vision.

Method: KPI Selection & Definition

1. REVIEW OBJECTIVES

⊛ For each objective, what metric(s) would indicate progress or achievement?

2. ENSURE MEASURABILITY

⊛ Can the KPI be measured accurately and consistently over time?

⊛ Identify the data sources and tools needed for measurement.

3. SET TARGETS

⊛ For each KPI, define specific, time-bound performance targets.

KPI GUIDANCE

1. **Lead vs Lag measures:** Leading indicators drive outcomes vs lagging outputs.
2. **Impact vs Vanity:** Tie KPIs directly to objectives; avoid "gaming".
3. **SMART criteria:** Specific, Measurable, Achievable, Relevant, Time-bound.

KPI TEMPLATE

Name - Definition - Data Source - Frequency - Target - Owner - Calculation Method

1. **Name:** Short label that identifies the KPI.

2. **Definition:** High-level description of exactly what the metric measures.

3. **Data Source:** Where the data will be pulled from - e.g. CRM system, surveys, ERP system.

4. **Frequency:** How regularly it will be measured - daily, weekly, monthly, quarterly etc.

5. **Target:** The specific performance threshold or goal to be achieved.

6. **Owner:** Person responsible for tracking + acting on the KPI.

7. **Calculation Method:** Exact formula for measuring/computing the KPI.

FOR EXAMPLE:

1. **Name:** Customer Satisfaction Score

2. **Definition:** Metric gauging satisfaction rating from customer surveys.

3. **Data Source:** Salesforce surveys.

4. **Frequency:** Quarterly

5. **Target:** Minimum score of 4.5 out of 5.

6. **Owner:** Customer Experience Manager.

7. **Calculation:** Average rating from the "Overall Satisfaction" question in customer post-purchase surveys

This template ensures all key elements are covered so that the KPIs driving performance towards strategic objectives are specific, measurable, and actionable.

KEY TAKEAWAYS

1. Crafted vision statement grounded in organizational values and aligned to situation and trends.

2. Established KPIs to track progress on strategic goals.

TAKE IT FURTHER

1. Now that you have defined the vision and KPIs, ensure they are effectively communicated throughout the organization.

2. Regularly review progress against KPIs and adjust objectives as needed to stay on track towards the vision.

3. Keep your vision and KPIs visible (e.g., posters, websites, workspaces, scoreboards, monitors) to foster a culture of alignment and motivate team members in pursuit of the shared goal.

VENTURE (V)

The Venture element empowers organizations to swiftly progress from planning to execution with flexible roadmaps that activate agile strategy.

"Venture forth with purpose, picking the paths of utmost priority."

OVERVIEW

The Venture exercise maps the strategic path forward by identifying and prioritizing initiatives, projects and actions needed to achieve the vision and objectives. This creates a roadmap for execution that nests current actions in alignment with future goals.

RETURN ON INVESTMENT (ROI) OF VENTURE (V)

Mapping the Venture element of STRIVE crystallizes the strategic path forward drawing a critical path from the current state, through the vision established in Intent. Rigorously identifying and prioritizing key initiatives and actions creates a blueprint for execution. Venture action plans also enable teams to sequence and stage activities for optimal returns. Rather than just lofty ideas, this element provides an actionable roadmap to activate strategy.

ACTIVATING STRATEGY WITH VENTURE

The "Venture" component of STRIVE is exciting; it embodies strategic application through intentional action, ensuring that each deliberate step contributes meaningfully towards the greater vision. But what makes purpose-driven venturing so essential? The answer can be found in examining diverse sectors like business, psychology, education, and the military. Each of which underscores the need for decisive action once clear Intent is defined. Let us review some examples:

1. **Business:** Amazon's diversification from e-commerce giant to a formidable player in cloud computing with AWS is a classic tale of business venturing done right. Instead of being confined to its primary industry, Amazon recognized and pursued a new avenue—cloud services. This was not a random endeavor but a calculated risk, underpinned by strategic vision, leading to significant profitability. The message? Clear strategic ventures, rooted in robust analysis, pave the way to unparalleled success.

2. **Psychology:** Delving into psychology, every behavior springs from an underlying intent. Dr. Edwin Locke's Goal Setting Theory accentuates this, emphasizing that clear and challenging goals bolster motivation and uplift performance. Venturing is not solely about movement; it is about movement with purpose, fortified by well-defined objectives. Such an approach is not merely a business stratagem; it is a psychological tenet that supercharges achievement.

3. **Education:** In designing trajectories for learning, curriculum architects do not just define the end game—like mastering a subject. They meticulously delineate the journey to reach that mastery. Each step in this educational venture strives for optimal utilization of resources, guiding learners systematically towards their final objective. In essence, purposeful venturing is as vital in academic corridors as it is in corporate boardrooms.

4. **Military:** Military operations are incredible examples of strategic venturing. Consider the D-Day invasion during WWII. The Allied forces did not just have a goal; they had a sequenced strategy nested in within their Intent—from initial air raids to climactic beach landings. Every phase was a calculated venture, ensuring that each strategic action set the stage for the next, inching closer to victory. Whether planning warfare or business moves, sequence, nested within actionable strategy are paramount.

IN CONCLUSION

Vision without action is a dormant dream abandoned to die, while unbridled action without vision can lead one astray. The Venture component of STRIVE is the bridge—connecting the vision to its tangible realization. But it is not about mere movement; it is about intentional action, clarity, and, above all, purpose.

VENTURE (V) EXERCISE

Purpose: To chart out a strategic path forward, ensuring that initiatives align with the overarching vision, and prioritize actions to maximize value and align with available resources.

EXERCISE 1:
STRATEGIC ACTION IDENTIFICATION

Objective: Brainstorm and create a prioritized list of strategic actions needed to achieve the short-term objectives and long-term vision that was crafted in Intent.

Method: Collaborative Action Mapping

1. BRAINSTORM OBJECTIVES (MILESTONES)

⊖ Create a list of the immediate, and near-term projects that need to be accomplished to begin moving in the direction of the new vision.

2. NARROW DOWN THE OPTIONS

⊖ If the list generated is extensive (more than 9 items), have each stakeholder rate all initiatives on a scale from 1-10, where 1 is the least impactful and 10 is the most impactful. Move the 9 items with the highest sum rating to exercise 2, migrate the others to a Long-Term Issues list for reevaluation later, or discard them now.

EXERCISE 2:
VALUE-DRIVEN PRIORITIZATION MATRIX

Objective: Rank strategic actions by critically evaluating their prospective impact against execution feasibility.

Method: Impact-Feasibility Matrix

1. **DETERMINE IMPACT**
   - For each action, assess its potential impact on the company's goals (High, Medium, Low).

2. **ASSESS FEASIBILITY**
   - Evaluate how feasible it is to execute the action considering resources, time, and constraints (High, Medium, Low).

3. **PLOT ON MATRIX**
   - Use a 3x3 grid. The vertical axis represents Impact, and the horizontal axis represents Feasibility.
   - Example Matrix

	LOW FEASIBILITY	MEDIUM FEASIBILITY	HIGH FEASIBILITY
High Impact			
Medium Impact			
Low Impact			

EXERCISE 3:
SMART / ER GOAL SETTING

Objective: Transform High Priority Objectives into SMART / ER Goals.

Method: SMART / ER Goal Setting

SMART / ER GOAL SETTING

1. **SET SMART/ER OBJECTIVES**
   - Create objectives that are clear, actionable, and have a set timeline.
      - Note: SMART/ER = Specific, Measurable, Attainable, Realistic, Time Bound / Ethical, Equitable, and Environmentally Sound
      - Note: Initially, focus on the three objectives with the highest prioritization rating. After these are complete, assess available resources to determine how many may be actioned simultaneously.

KEY TAKEAWAYS

1. Identified and documented key strategic objectives and actions.
2. Prioritized objectives based on impact and feasibility analysis.
3. Transformed objectives into SMART /ER goals that will act as milestones towards vision attainment.
4. Created executable roadmap linking actions to strategic objectives, that can be updated as you proceed.

TAKE IT FURTHER:

1. For actions that are high impact but less feasible, consider allocating resources or finding ways to increase feasibility.
2. Regularly review and adjust actions as circumstances change, ensuring they remain aligned with objectives and vision.

ENGAGE (E)

ENABLE CONTINUOUS ADAPTATION

Embedding Engage into workflows fosters an iterative culture of learning and adaptation, powering the agility to continuously evolve and grow.

"Engage in continuous feedback, collaborate efficiently, and adapt when necessary."

OVERVIEW

The Engage element is the critical continuous improvement, consistency and accountability forcing function as it puts in place the mechanisms to sustain strategic change through feedback channels, collaboration tools and regular stakeholder reviews. This enables adaptation in response to rapidly shifting dynamics and ensures successful change management.

RETURN ON INVESTMENT (ROI) OF ENGAGE (E)

Embedding Engage into workflows fosters rapid learning and adaptation which is key to resilience. Continuous stakeholder feedback, real-time data, and regular strategy reviews enable live course correction versus rigid plan adherence. Engage also operationalizes successful change management through tools like prototyping and iteration.

THE PIVOTAL ROLE OF ENGAGE: CONTINUING THE JOURNEY

Continuous, iterative engagement is perhaps the most critical component of the STRIVE framework, as it is the forcing function that keeps all our efforts up to this point alive. And it is the element that fortifies, adjusts, and helps your team to go the distance, and accomplish your Intent by protecting, fueling, and adjusting how you Venture as informed by your Situation, current Trends, and the Risks that you continue to navigate. It underscores deep, consistent, and meaningful involvement. The necessity of engagement is not restricted to one domain but resonates across multiple sectors. Exploring multiple sectors uncovers the undeniable importance of the 'Engage' element of STRIVE.

EXAMPLES:

1. **Business:** In business, the Agile methodology emerges as a shining example of the profound impact of engagement. Rather than merely concentrating on software production, Agile places paramount importance on iterative development, ongoing feedback, and adaptive evolution. Teams operate within "sprints" – concise development cycles – where they create functional software components. These components are then honed and refined in subsequent sprints, influenced by the feedback received. This mode of operation underscores a pivotal insight: Just as the Agile model thrives on recurrent feedback and continual adaptation, effective business engagement necessitates a similar approach, constantly realigning strategies to resonate with the ever-shifting business terrain while ensuring they continue to be prioritized appropriately.

2. **Education and Psychology:** In educational psychology, formative assessments stand out as pivotal tools that prioritize continuous feedback throughout the learning process. Rather than relegating evaluations to the term's end, these assessments offer regular insights, ensuring that educators can make timely instructional adjustments to enhance the learning experience. Drawing a parallel, just as formative assessments are built on the bedrock of continuous feedback, the 'Engage' principle in the STRIVE methodology underscores the significance of routine evaluations and fine-tuning. This approach not only identifies areas of improvement but also fosters an environment primed for achieving optimal outcomes.

3. **Military:** Drawing inspiration from military strategies, the OODA loop, an acronym for "Observe, Orient, Decide, Act," stands as a testament to dynamic decision-making, especially during intense combat situations. This brainchild of strategist John Boyd emphasizes a cyclical process where soldiers are encouraged to consistently observe their environment, align their strategies, make informed decisions, and then act. After every action, they revisit the observation phase, ensuring that strategies adapt and evolve based on real-time conditions. Drawing a parallel with strategic engagement, just as the OODA loop underscores continuous re-evaluation and action, the 'Engage' facet in strategic frameworks accentuates the value of perpetual reassessment and nimble adaptation, especially when navigating unpredictable scenarios.

4. **Healthcare:** Within healthcare, the Patient-Centered Medical Home (PCMH) model has emerged as a paradigm of holistic patient care. Designed to put patients at the heart of their treatment, PCMH emphasizes an environment where continuous communication is interwoven with care processes. It not only values and integrates feedback from patients but also champions collaborative efforts among healthcare professionals, ensuring that care is coordinated, comprehensive, and tailored to individual needs. Mirroring this approach, the 'Engage' principle underscores that, just as in healthcare, open channels of communication and regular feedback are pivotal in sustaining progress for well-crafted strategies that yield outstanding outcomes.

IN CONCLUSION

The doctrine of engagement, championed by STRIVE, reverberates across a myriad of industries. The agile flexibility in business, the feedback-focused academic approach, the swift military adaptability, or the cooperative spirit in healthcare - all converge to one foundational truth: For victory in every venture, unwavering engagement, feedback, intentionality, and adaptability are critical. The Engage element of STRIVE encapsulates this need, urging us to not just plan, but to continually act, adapt, and evolve.

ENGAGE (E) EXERCISES

Purpose: Cultivate an environment of iterative feedback, seamless collaboration, and proactive strategy adaptation.

EXERCISE 1:
FEEDBACK CHANNEL ESTABLISHMENT

Objective: Establish clear, easy-to-use feedback channels for stakeholders.

Method: Feedback Channel Mapping

1. ### CONFIRM / IDENTIFY STAKEHOLDERS

    → Given this, list all the internal and external stakeholders involved in or affected by your strategy. Identify which ones will be included in throughout the iterative feedback process.

    → If this is step is actioned during the workshop, or with the support of Iron Front, we are likely in the same room as the primary Stakeholders, however we may be missing some. Additionally, some of those here may only be involved in the establishment of the organizations Intent, and therefore will not hold an ongoing seat of responsibility in its application.

2. ### CHOOSE FEEDBACK MECHANISMS

    → Decide the feedback tools or channels for each stakeholder. This could range from surveys to regular meetings to digital feedback platforms. Choose simple, straightforward tools or channels ensuring maximum response.

→ Iron Front Solutions strongly recommends echeloned weekly meetings to review KPIs, and ensure progress is being made in line with the established SMART/ER Goals, Objectives, Milestones, and the Vision. This also allows for shifts in operating procedures and other related changes that will likely need to occur as your team evolves to accomplish each objective.

3. DOCUMENT CHANNELS

→ Record the chosen mechanisms and ensure they are accessible to the primary stakeholders. Clearly communicate the feedback mechanism, frequency of feedback, and its importance to the primary stakeholders and team members.

EXERCISE 2:
COLLABORATION TOOL INTEGRATION

Objective: Optimize team cohesion and project efficiency by identifying and utilizing the best collaboration tools.

Method: Collaboration Tool Assessment

1. **LIST EXISTING TOOLS**
   - ➔ Document all the collaboration tools currently being used by your team or organization.

2. **ASSESS EFFECTIVENESS**
   - ➔ Evaluate the effectiveness of each tool. Is it serving its purpose? Are there any gaps?

3. **RECOMMENDED TOOLS**
   - ➔ Iron Front provides Asana based task management and meeting templated solutions that will facilitate this process, and if desired, we can aid you with the digitization of your team as well. Please reach out if this is of interest.

EXERCISE 3:
ADAPTIVE STRIVE REVIEW

Objective: Regularly review the current strategy considering feedback and emerging changes, adapting as necessary using the STRIVE Methodology.

Method: Quarterly STRIVE Review Meetings

1. **COMPILE FEEDBACK**
    - ➲ Review STRIVE produced outputs and ensure they are coherent and up to date. This should include recently gathered feedback from the organization (such as skip level feedback, surveys, etc.) to ensure that the Situation, Trends, and Risks elements of STRIVE are fully informing your teams review of Intent and Venture.

2. **EVALUATE STRATEGY**
    - ➲ Assess the strategy's effectiveness given:
        - ➲ Are objectives being met?
        - ➲ Are there any new challenges or opportunities?
        - ➲ What has changed from Situation, Trends, and Risks that can help us to better engage in our pursuit of our Intent?

3. **ADAPT AND MODIFY**
    - ➲ Based on feedback and evaluation, make necessary modifications to the strategy to ensure it remains effective and relevant.
    - ➲ Note: Adjustments done as a result of this meeting should be sourced from the reevaluation of your circumstances from STRIVE. Otherwise, issues and inefficiencies should have been adjusted in real time. If this is not the case, please speak with your Iron Front Executive Consultant.

KEY TAKEAWAYS

1. Established feedback channels to enable continuous stakeholder engagement.

2. Assessed and optimized collaboration tools to enhance team coordination.

3. Instituted regular reviews to adapt strategy based on insights and changes.

TAKE IT FURTHER

1. Cultivate an empowered environment of individual leadership where feedback is not only encouraged but aggressively acted upon.

2. Regularly evaluate collaboration tools to ensure that they are serving your teams effectively, and that your team is using the tool.

3. Be prepared to adapt your Intent and with it your priorities, staying agile and responsive to the ever-evolving business landscape is critical to accomplish your teams' long-term goals.

REALIZING THE FULL POTENTIAL OF STRIVE

The STRIVE methodology provides more than a strategic planning process —it outlines a pathway for organizations to progress from static plans to continuous, agile leadership.

At its core, STRIVE is designed to become deeply embedded into an enterprise's culture and workflows. This enables the principles of intentionality, adaptation, and insight to permeate decision making at all levels.

To activate STRIVE's full potential requires investment in building dynamic capabilities across teams. This includes equipping them with frameworks to rapidly prototype ideas using customer-driven experiments and feedback loops.

The intent is to foster a fail-fast, learn-faster culture that turns uncertainty into an advantage. By cementing these concepts into everyday operations, organizations can uphold their core purpose amidst external turbulence.

As we conclude our exploration of STRIVE, one truth stands clear: this methodology offers an immense opportunity to reshape how enterprises navigate uncertainty and disruption.

Strategic resilience is available to you. Should you commit to embedding this culture, one milestone will lead to the next. One pilot will build upon the last. One small win will compound into enterprise-wide transformation. And suddenly, achieving mastery amidst chaos will not be a matter of happenstance but a reality forged by choice. The future will be yours to own rather than endure.

The principles are in place. Now the decision is yours to make.

Are you ready?

NEXT STEPS

THANK YOU FOR READING
STRIVE: MASTER STRATEGY
WITH AGILITY.

TO LEARN MORE, CHECK OUT
HTTPS://JONMAYO.COM

.

www.ingramcontent.com/pod-product-compliance
Lightning Source LLC
Chambersburg PA
CBHW052142270326
41930CB00012B/2984